Invest in Yourself
Developing Skills that Pay Off

Table of Contents

Chapter 1. Introduction

Embrace the power of personal growth with our Special Report: "Invest in Yourself: Developing Skills that Pay Off". This extraordinary guide artfully blends knowledge, real-life examples, and inspiration – providing an exciting journey to enhance your personal and professional life. Not overly technical, it focuses on areas of self-improvement that are both accessible and highly impactful. You'll learn to identify and cultivate skills that are in high demand, subsequently offering not only occupational advantages but success spilling over into every aspect of your life. Whether you're a student exploring future opportunities or a professional embarking on a new phase of your career, this Special Report will reignite your passion for learning and inspire a commitment to personal evolution. Secure your copy today, and let the journey to a better version of you begin!

Chapter 2. Unleashing Your Potential: An Introduction

We all possess an innate potential within us. It's like a dormant volcano waiting for the right moment to erupt and show the world its fiery brilliance. Throughout our lives, we allow only a fraction of this potential to shine through. The rest, we either suppress or do not recognize. But what would happen if we decided to tap into this reservoir of skills and abilities?

2.1. Unearthing Hidden Skills

The first step towards unleashing your potential is to acknowledge its existence. Recognizing dormant skills can be a formidable challenge, as they can often lurk behind our daily routines and perceived shortcomings. One way to unearth hidden abilities is by extending your curiosity towards everything around you. Endeavor to learn something new each day, accept new challenges and test uncharted territories.

Reflect on your journey, experiences, passions, and draw a circle around them. Your skills are most likely encapsulated in this circle. It could be anything from problem-solving, critical thinking, artistry, team management to more uncommon skills like lucid dreaming or cross-pollinating ideas. Once these hidden skills are identified, they act as a compass, helping guide your further personal and professional development.

2.2. The Power of Self-Belief

Choosing to believe in yourself and your abilities is vital. This initiation into self-belief can often be a leap of faith - but it is a leap worth taking. Trust in your capacity to learn, grow and succeed.

Understand that failures, setbacks, and drawbacks are not endpoints but rather stepping stones that contribute to your journey of growth.

Self-belief is about recognizing your value, potential, and worth. It requires acceptance of where you are and a vision for where you could be. Moreover, it involves turning this vision into tangible action steps.

2.3. Growth Mindset: A Catalyst for Success

Adopting a growth mindset is critical in your journey towards personal evolution. It encourages the thought that abilities and understanding can be developed. Those with a growth mindset believe in possibilities and improvement through effort. They comprehend that effort is not just a means to an end but also constitutes the core of development and achievement.

A growth mindset changes your attitude towards failure by reframing it as an opportunity to learn and evolve. It fuels resilience and sparks drive in the face of challenges. This mentality is not about being the best; it's about constantly becoming better.

2.4. Building on Your Strengths

Your strengths are your power, and leveraging them is fundamental. By knowing what we are naturally good at, we can focus our efforts in areas where we will reap the most rewards. There is a greater sense of satisfaction and productivity when we operate in our zones of strength, breeding not only success but happiness as well.

Choosing to build on your strengths does not mean ignoring your weaknesses. Instead, it means you're optimizing your potential by directing your resources where they'll have the greatest impact. Then you can develop strategies to manage any weaknesses.

2.5. Lifelong Learning: The Key to Adaptability

In a rapidly changing world, adaptability is a premium trait, and with lifelong learning, you can cultivate this trait. Lifelong learning promotes the constant updating and expansion of your skillset, allowing you to adapt to new circumstances, challenges, and technologies. It embodies a sincere love for learning, transforming it from a chore into something enjoyable and rewarding.

From reading books, attending webinars, and workshops, to pursuing additional qualifications, there are countless ways you can commit to lifelong learning.

2.6. Conclusion

Unleashing your potential is a journey of discovery and growth. It involves exploring your hidden talents, adopting a growth mindset, and harnessing your strengths. As we develop our skills and embrace emerging opportunities, we can face the future with adaptability and confidence.

Therefore, don't underestimate your potential, for you are capable of astonishing things. It's time to recognize this, let that potential take flight, and inspire others with your journey. This is the true power of personal and professional evolution.

Chapter 3. Identifying Your Strengths: The Importance of Self-Knowledge

Self-knowledge is often considered an ethical and philosophical concept, but its importance in personal and professional growth cannot be overstated. Knowing yourself is the first step towards understanding what you are truly capable of, and how to exploit these capabilities to achieve your goals. This forms the bedrock of self-improvement around which you can structure your learning and development initiatives.

3.1. The Mirror of Self-Reflection

The journey towards self-knowledge starts with the act of self-reflection. It is through reflection that we can gaze into the mirror of our own thoughts, feelings, and experiences. To do this, we need to set aside some time for introspection. This is often easier said than done in our fast-paced world, which is why a committed approach is necessary to ensuring that self-reflection becomes part of our routine.

During self-reflection, we should ask ourselves questions about our life experiences. What did we learn from them? How did they make us feel? How did they shape our perspective? By addressing these questions, we can begin to develop a comprehensive understanding of our strengths and weaknesses.

3.2. Tools for Self-Reflection

Multiple tools can aid in your process of self-reflection. From assessments and quizzes to journals and signaling tools, choose a method that resonates with your style of thinking. Journaling, for instance, is a powerful method that can help organize your thoughts, monitor your mental patterns over a period, and discover trends in your behavior and decision-making.

Completing psychological assessments, like Myers-Briggs Type Indicator (MBTI), StrengthsFinder, or Emotional Quotient Inventory (EQ-i), can provide insights into your personality traits, emotional responses, and mental capacities—strengths that you might not have been aware of.

3.3. Discovering Your Strengths

Your strengths are the characteristics, skills, and qualities that make you unique and effective in particular situations. They are typically associated with activities or tasks that you can do well and that you enjoy. But how do you identify your strengths?

One practical approach is to keep a 'strengths journal,' where you keep track of activities or moments when you felt most energetic, satisfied, or accomplished. Look for patterns among these experiences. Perhaps you excel in social situations, or maybe your strengths lie in problem-solving under pressure. Identify these patterns and document them.

Additionally, you can receive feedback from those who know you well—friends, family, colleagues, mentors. Their insights might provide a different perspective on your strengths, revealing aspects of your behaviors or skillsets that you may not have noticed yourself.

3.4. Strengths and Skills: The Difference

Strengths and skills are often used interchangeably but understanding the difference between the two can provide more clarity during the self-exploration journey. Strengths are innate, something that you are naturally good at. For instance, being empathetic or industrious can be considered strengths.

On the other hand, skills are acquired through learning and practice. They involve the application of knowledge and can be learned or improved over time, such as writing, coding, or public speaking.

3.5. Link Between Strengths and High-Demand Skills

Combining your strengths with high-demand skills can pave a successful path toward a lucrative and satisfying career. High-demand skills are abilities sought after by employers across various industries,such as leadership, communication, critical thinking or technological prowess. These skills address organizations' ongoing needs and changes in the business landscape.

To link strengths with high-demand skills, identify the commonalities between your natural abilities and those skills. For instance, if you're a natural leader and organization is a strength of yours, you could seek to cultivate project management skills, a highly demanded ability in many sectors.

3.6. Gaming the Advantage

Knowing your strengths and investing your time to develop corresponding high-demand skills can pay dividends, not only to your career growth but also your personal growth. Through a targeted approach to skill development, you can maximize the return on your time invested, leading to accelerated advancement and increased job satisfaction.

In conclusion, self-knowledge forms the foundation upon which personal and professional development is built. It's a gold mine of insights into your natural abilities and potential areas of growth. The more you know about yourself and your strengths, the better equipped you are to navigate through life and achieve your version of success. Start your journey of self-discovery today—lookup, reflect, and let your strengths guide your way!

Chapter 4. Learning New Skills: A Roadmap

Before we delve into the intricacies of acquiring new skills, let's remind ourselves of an old adage – "Learning is a journey, not a destination." It's an ongoing process that continues throughout our lives, shaping us into more versatile and adaptable individuals. Now, let's explore this exciting journey of acquiring new skills structured under several sub-chapters.

4.1. Identifying Your Interests and Strengths

When starting the journey toward learning a new skill, your interests and strengths should serve as your guideposts. You're naturally inclined to be invested and excel in areas where you have a vested interest.

To identify your interests:

- Start by listing your hobbies, passions, and activities you enjoy

- Reflect on past experiences, projects, or jobs in which you felt most vital and effective

- Rely on self-assessment tools available online

Knowing your strengths is equally crucial:

- Reflection and introspection can aid in understanding your strengths

- Feedback from peers, colleagues, and mentors can offer valuable insights

- Strength finding instruments such as CliftonStrengths can be helpful resources

Remember, your interests and strengths can help unveil promising skill pathways worth exploring.

4.2. Setting Specific, Measurable, Achievable, Relevant, Time-bound (SMART) Goals

With a clear understanding of which skills you want to acquire, developing SMART goals can channel your efforts effectively, thereby fostering an efficient learning process.

- Specific: Have a clear, well-defined goal for the skill you wish to learn

- Measurable: Determine how you'll gauge progress

- Achievable: Ensure that acquiring the new skill is doable

- Relevant: Verify that the skill aligns with your interests and career goals

- Time-bound: Set a deadline for achieving competency in the skill

Goals formulated based on these parameters can enhance your commitment to learning and fuel your journey toward mastering new skills.

4.3. Finding the Right Learning Resources

The availability of diverse resources in today's digital world has made self-learning more feasible than ever.

- Traditional Courses: These offer structured curriculums and benefit those drawn to more formalized education settings

- Online Learning Platforms: Websites like Coursera, edX, and Skillshare provide broad access to high-quality content

- Books and Ebooks: These remain timeless resources for in-depth exploration and understanding

- Podcasts and Webinars: These provide dynamic, flexible ways to learn new skills

- Networking and Mentoring: Connecting with mentors and peers can impart insights that traditional courses may not offer

Out of these, choose the avenue that appeals to your learning style.

4.4. Active Learning and Practicing

Accumulating knowledge is insufficient. We must actively engage in the application and practice of what we learn. Applying these measures can help:

- Active Listening and Reading: Engage with the content and strive to truly understand the concepts

- Notes Making: Use techniques like the Cornell method or Mind-mapping for effective note-taking

- Regular Practice: Increase your proficiency with routine practice sessions

- Real-World Application: Apply your skills to real-world scenarios

Understand that the key to mastering a skill lies in the mantra – practice, process, and persist.

4.5. Dealing with Potential Roadblocks

Skill acquisition isn't always a smooth sail. You may encounter challenges and obstacles along the way. However, overcoming them can lead to significant growth.

- Fear of Failure: Understand that failure is part of learning. Embrace it as a stepping stone to success

- Lack of Time: Break down your learning journey into manageable chunks of time

- Losing Motivation: Remember your initial excitement and the value the new skill adds to your life

With grit and determination, you can navigate through these roadblocks and continue on your rewarding journey.

4.6. Evaluating Progress and Continuous Learning

The final step in the roadmap of learning a new skill is evaluating your progress and ensuring continuous learning. Regular check-ins on your progress help identify areas of improvement.

Meanwhile, once you have achieved a degree of proficiency in a new skill, seek opportunities to share your knowledge. Teaching others is a great way to solidify what you've learned. Furthermore, accept that learning is never-ending. Keep exploring new horizons and continue with the cycle of learning, practicing, and evaluating.

By this point, you should have a comprehensive understanding of the intricate journey to learning new skills. Remember, it's your effort, dedication, and desire for self-improvement that will fuel this journey. Stay committed, resilient, and curious during your quest for personal growth. Rest assured that the returns on this valuable investment will be manifold, enriching both your personal and professional life.

13

Chapter 5. Time Management: Balancing Growth and Life

There is a simple yet profound axiom that states, "Time is money." In the fiercely competitive world of today, the ability to manage one's time effectively is a skill that can yield rich dividends. In this chapter, we will delve into the critical area of time management, exploring strategies for maintaining a healthy balance between personal growth and a fulfilling life, presented within the following sub-chapters.

5.1. The Value of Time in Personal Development

Time is an irreplaceable asset that we sometimes undervalue. Each minute that passes is a minute that we can't get back. When it comes to personal development or self-improvement, every moment dedicated counts significantly. Using our time wisely helps us get closer to our goals.

The first step to time management is introspection, and recognizing how you currently spend your time. A simple, yet effective tool, a 'Time Audit' – where tracking your activities over a week will provide a clear picture of your current time utilization. Note the time spent on various activities, particularly those that do not contribute to your personal growth, and assess where you could save some minutes.

5.2. Setting Priorities for Growth

Once you have an understanding of your current time utilization, the next step is to prioritize your activities. Prioritizing helps us focus on what's essential, allowing more time to devote to our personal growth.

Begin by listing down all your daily and weekly tasks, and then segregate them into 4 categories: urgent and important; important but not urgent; urgent but not important; and not urgent or important. This is known as the Eisenhower matrix, a highly effective method to separate your actions based on urgency and importance.

5.3. Strategies for Effective Time Management

Having prioritized your tasks, it's time to develop strategies to manage them effectively.

- **Plan Ahead**: Planning is the essence of time management. Use planners, calendars, or apps to plan your activities in advance. Be sure to allocate enough time for personal growth activities.

- **Time Blocking**: Dedicate specific time blocks during the day for specific tasks. This ensures that each activity has an allotted time, reducing the chance of procrastination.

- **The Pomodoro Technique**: This involves working for a set amount of time (usually 25 minutes) and then taking a short break (5 minutes). After every four 'Pomodoros', take a longer break.

- **Say No When Necessary**: It's okay to say no to requests or activities that are not in line with your personal growth path.

5.4. Balancing Personal Growth and Life

It's crucial to remember that while self-development is important, so too are other areas of life, such as health, relationships, and leisure.

To achieve a balance, integrate your personal growth objectives into your daily life rather than treating them as separate. For instance, if communication skills are part of your personal growth plan, practice them in your everyday interactions.

5.5. Overcoming Time Management Challenges

Even with proper planning and strategies, you may find challenges. Overcoming these hurdles is a process that requires adaptability and patience.

When interruptions occur, adjust your schedule and return to your tasks as soon as possible. If certain tasks consume more time than anticipated, evaluate whether to continue investing in them or consider alternate ways to achieve your goal. Above all, always save buffer time for unexpected delays and disruptions.

5.6. Reviewing Your Time Management Approach

Just like any other skill, time management also requires regular review and refinement. Keep checking your progress, reassess your priorities, and make necessary adjustments in your strategies and plans.

Remember, effective time management isn't about getting more things done, but about getting the right things done. It's about recognizing that time is a finite resource and thus needs to be spent wisely, towards accomplishing your self-improvement goals, while also living a fulfilling life.

Despite its challenges, successful time management brings numerous rewards. As Benjamin Franklin aptly put it, "Do you love life? Then do not squander time, for that's the stuff life is made of." So, invest in it wisely, balancing personal growth with a rich, vibrant life.

Chapter 6. Continuing Education: The Perks and Practicalities

In this swiftly changing job landscape, we are witnessing an increased premium being placed on those who avail themselves of continuing education opportunities. Acquiring fresh skills, refining existing competencies, or learning about new industries not only significantly bolster your resume but also provide a genuine sense of accomplishment and growth.

6.1. Understanding Continuing Education

Continuing education refers to the pursuit of knowledge beyond an individual's formal educational years. Whether it's specialized training courses, certificate programs, conferences, workshops, webinars, or self-paced online learning — continuing education aids in keeping your skillset sharp and relevant. Conversations about personal and professional development remain incomplete without acknowledging the key role continuing education plays.

Though a bachelor's degree or initial professional training might provide the groundwork for a career, it's the act of ongoing learning that keeps you agile in a dynamic work ecosystem. Industries evolve with time, new trends surface, and technologies get replaced. Continuing education empowers individuals to stay in step with these shifts.

6.2. Benedictions of Continuing Education

Continuing education is multifaceted in its perks, with benefits extending beyond mere professional advancement.

6.2.1. An Edge in a Competitive Job Market

The modern job market is saturated, and possessing unique skills or knowledge can set you apart from others. By showcasing your commitment to learning and evolving, you signal to potential employers that you're an initiative-taker, eager to adapt and grow.

6.2.2. Better Job Prospects and Promotion Opportunities

Relevant additional qualifications open doors to new opportunities. Employees who complete continuing education programs often find themselves presented with advancement options within their organizations, helping them scale the corporate ladder faster.

6.2.3. Lifetime Learning and Personal Fulfillment

Pursuing formalized continuing education enforces a mindset of lifelong learning. This does not only provide an immense sense of personal satisfaction but also contributes to improved self-esteem and a significant increase in adaptability.

6.3. Seeing Through the Practical Lens

While the advantages of continuing education seem compelling, it's essential to scrutinize the practicalities involved too.

6.3.1. Time and Commitment

Continuing education often requires a certain time commitment, which varies depending on the course type you opt for. Time management becomes crucial, especially for working professionals where fitting in continuing education could mean spending personal or family time.

6.3.2. Financial Investment

Continuing education is an investment in oneself, which often has a financial component to it. This is an aspect to consider when selecting the type of continuing education program one wishes to engage in. Scholarships, employer assistance schemes, or self-paced online courses could be worthwhile avenues worth exploring when expenses come into play.

6.3.3. Choosing the Right Program

Not all continuing education programs are created equal. One must carry out ample research, reflect on career goals, consider the time factor, and seek advice before making an informed decision.

6.4. Wrapping Up

A world where qualifications perish quickly, and new skills become prerequisites overnight requires an individual to be proactive. Embarking on the path of continuing education is an investment that seldom stands unrewarded. It enhances one's professional recognition, personal growth, network expansion, and ultimately, serves as a stepping stone to a more fulfilling career and life. It remains, truly, a decision that begins with you, for you.

Chapter 7. Networking and Mentorship: Cultivating Valuable Connections

There's a universal adage that permeates diverse cultures worldwide: "It's not what you know, it's who you know." This statement underscores the crucial importance of our social networks in achieving our goals.

In personal and professional environments alike, networking shapes the trajectory of our lives in undeniable ways. It opens doors to opportunities, accelerates learning, infuses fresh perspectives, and propels individuals' and teams' advancements.

This chapter will delve deep into the world of networking and mentorship, exposing you to the influences they could have on your journey towards personal and professional growth.

7.1. The Essence of Networking

Networking is the active process of creating and nurturing professional relationships. It's about establishing connections with individuals or groups who share common purposes or interests. But networking isn't just about accumulating a vast number of connections; it's about fostering strong and quality relationships that could eventually push you forward in life.

These relationships can come in various forms. You may have a connection with someone in your work environment, your professional association, your online interactions, or your social connections. Each of these connections has a potential to impact your life in meaningful ways. They could offer you fresh perspectives, new discoveries, valuable advice, exposure to opportunities, and even encouragement in your times of stress.

7.2. Building Your Network

When it comes to networking, it's essential to have a clear and focused approach. Be intentional about your networking activities. Start by identifying the key people or groups you'd like to connect with and then develop a strategy to reach out to them.

There's a wide range of approaches you can take. You could start by joining a professional association, attending conferences or seminars, or by actively participating in online forums or social media discussions around your interests. Remember, networking is not only about receiving benefits; it also involves giving back. Be willing to offer help, share advice, or contribute your expertise when possible.

Building your network also requires you to step out of your comfort zone. Don't be afraid of initiating conversations, meeting new people, or expressing your ideas. Show genuine interest in others and listen actively when they speak. These actions are vital elements in establishing strong connections.

However, networking isn't an instant process. It's a long-term investment that requires time, patience, consistency, and nurturing. Don't be discouraged if you don't see immediate results; focus on fostering relationships and the benefits will naturally follow.

7.3. The Role of Mentorship

In addition to networking, mentorship is another powerful tool for personal and professional advancement. A mentor is someone who offers insights, guidance, and support based on their wealth of experience. They can assist you in navigating complicated paths, avoiding pitfalls, and making informed decisions.

But perhaps the most significant advantage of mentorship is the opportunity for personal development. When mentors share their experiences, they also divulite valuable life lessons that inspire growth. Such shared wisdom is crucial for emotional, personal, and professional development.

7.4. Choosing the Right Mentor

Selecting the right mentor is crucial, and it should be a careful decision. Look for qualities like compatibility, experience, knowledge in your area of interest, and willingness to share. Avoid rushing into mentorship relationships; take your time to understand the potential mentor's commitments and expectations.

Once you've chosen a mentor, it's up to you to make the most out of the relationship. Be open to feedback, willing to learn, respectful of your mentor's time, and always show gratitude for their assistance. Regularly communicate your ambitions and difficulties to your mentor. After all, the more they understand about you, the better they can guide you.

In conclusion, networking and mentorship serve as valuable assets in personal growth and professional development. These tools offer fresh perspectives, accelerate learning, and provide opportunities for advancement. They are the wheels that accelerate the journey towards becoming the best version of oneself. Implement these strategies, and you'll observe a significant change in the trajectory of your growth and success.

Chapter 8. Harnessing Technology: Your Pathway to Skill Enhancement

Technology: it's revolutionised our society, impacted virtually every aspect of life, and forayed into workplaces changing the way we work. Undeniably, it has emerged as a tool that can make a significant difference in our personal and professional growth, providing an indispensable pathway for skill enhancement.

8.1. What Does Harnessing Technology Mean Today?

In today's context, harnessing technology means keeping up-to-date with technological advancements and innovations. It involves understanding how various technologies work and how they can be used to solve problems or create opportunities. It is about leveraging technology to augment skills and abilities.

Technology is versatile and diverse, so harnessing it involves a wide array of skills. Some of the most crucial are digital literacy, technical knowledge, and adequate hands-on experience. But technology also involves a mindset: a willingness to constantly learn, adapt and innovate.

8.2. The Impact of Technological Advance on Skill Enhancement

The advent and advancement of technology have made skill enhancement a more streamlined and efficient process. Not only do technological tools aid in teaching, training, and developing skills in various fields, but they also open up opportunities to acquire new, relevant skills that can open doors professionally.

Consider online courses, simulations, and virtual reality; these provide unique, interactive learning environments where one can learn at their own pace. Through these tools, you can gain exposure to concepts and scenarios that might be difficult – or even impossible – to experience otherwise. They also foster a learner-centric approach that caters to individual learning styles and preferences.

8.3. Identifying Skills to Enhance

Understanding the technology landscape is a crucial step for skill enhancement. Network with industry professionals, join online communities and forums, and utilise online resources such as blogs and podcasts to gain insight into the latest tech trends and opportunities. Identify which technical skills are in demand in your industry or field of interest. These could include coding languages, software proficiency, data analysis, artificial intelligence, cybersecurity, or others. Then, align these skills with your personal interests and career goals for maximum benefit.

8.4. Building a Learning Plan

Once you've identified the tech skills you want to improve or acquire, build a learning plan. Consider your current skill level, learning style, available learning resources, and the time you can commit to learning. Web-based learning platforms—like Coursera, Udemy, or LinkedIn Learning—offer a plethora of courses on a wide range of tech skills. Allocate consistent, focused time for learning. Progress may be slow initially, but with persistence, it will speed up.

Remember, it's not just about completing a course or earning a certificate. The true measure of learning is being able to apply the knowledge and utilize the skills you've gained in real-life scenarios.

8.5. Embracing the Growth Mindset

A common theme you'll see when you start learning about technology is that the learning never stops. Technology evolves rapidly, and the most successful individuals in this realm are those who maintain a growth mindset, an understanding that abilities and intelligence can be developed.

Impatience, fear of failure, and a tendency to avoid challenges are all roadblocks on the path to learning. Cultivate a mindset that embraces challenges, persist in the face of setbacks, and understand that effort is the path to mastery.

8.6. Mentorship and Collaboration

Find a mentor to help navigate your learning journey. A mentor can offer guidance, feedback, and share their experiences, helping you avoid common pitfalls. Additionally, consider joining a community of learners. Collaborative learning environments can be incredibly rewarding, offering help when you're stuck, fostering discussions, and opening up networking opportunities.

Harnessing technology for skill enhancement is not a destination but a journey. It's about continual learning, adapting, and growing. As technology continues to evolve, remember that it's not about being a master, but a lifelong learner.

By leaning into technology, you're not just enhancing your skills for the present; you're preparing for a future that is increasingly digitized. You're investing in yourself, opening doors to opportunities, and moving towards a better version of yourself. Your pathway to skill enhancement awaits!

Chapter 9. Emotional Intelligence: The Unseen Skillset

Emotional Intelligence, often referred to as EQ, represents a combination of abilities that involve understanding, identifying, and managing emotions, ultimately contributing to superior self-understanding, relating to others, and making effective decisions.

9.1. Understanding Emotional Intelligence

Emotional Intelligence serves as a cornerstone for healthy interpersonal interactions. Along with cognitive intelligence (IQ), Emotional Intelligence complements an individual's overall intelligence portfolio. It's been found to be a strong predictor of both personal happiness and professional success.

Comprehending emotions can go beyond reading others — it's about understanding our own feelings and interpreting them to facilitate personal development. Understanding the triggers causing certain feelings can offer insights into personality traits and reaction patterns. Armed with such knowledge, one can better navigate personal relationships, workplace dynamics, decision-making, and future emotional landscapes.

9.2. Components of Emotional Intelligence

In exploring the realm of emotional intelligence, it's essential to consider its key components, as defined by psychologist Daniel

Goleman. He identifies the five pillars of EQ as self-awareness, self-regulation, motivation, empathy, and social skills. Each element complements and builds upon the other, creating a framework for meaningful, emotionally intelligent interaction.

1. **Self-Awareness**: Having a deep understanding of one's emotions and recognizing their impact on actions and reactions is the bedrock of emotional intelligence. Being cognizant of strengths and weaknesses can shape personal growth journeys, presenting opportunities for growth and the heightening of emotional wisdom.

2. **Self-Regulation**: It's about managing one's emotions, especially in stressful situations. An emotionally intelligent individual can control impulses and make conscious, thoughtful decisions that are in line with their ethical boundaries and personal or professional goals.

3. **Motivation**: Emotionally intelligent individuals tend to have a high degree of motivation, which makes them resilient and optimistic. The pursuit of goals is passion-driven rather than predominantly monetary or status-driven.

4. **Empathy**: Being able to recognize and understand emotions in others is a vital trait in developing relationships. Empathy encourages natural communicative flow and builds deeper connections with our peers. The ability to empathize often forms the basis for trust, making it essential in both professional and personal realms.

5. **Social Skills**: This component encapsulates capabilities to navigate social situations effectively. Skilled individuals engage naturally with others, manage disputes, and inspire positive interactions, all key ingredients for leadership.

9.3. Emotional intelligence and Personal Growth

Emotional Intelligence can significantly influence personal growth. Concordantly, as we evolve, our EQ can increase. Building emotional intelligence brings reciprocal benefits, impacting the personal sphere initially and, through that evolved sense of self, enhancing workplace culture, leadership skills and overall job performance.

Self-Development: The journey of personal growth heavily relies on the awareness of self, leveraging emotional intelligence to uncover innate potential. The practice of mindfulness can foster EQ, in turn powering a deeper understanding of consciousness.

Improving Relationships: Emotional intelligence can foster healthier communication, empathy and conflict resolution, forming a stronghold for robust relationships. By understanding not only our own emotions but the emotions of others, we can navigate relationships more tactfully and effectively.

Decision Making: Emotional intelligence vastly impacts our decision-making process. Understanding the emotional undertones of our choices can prevent impulsive decisions and lead to choices that align better with our objectives.

9.4. Emotional Intelligence in the Professional Landscape

Emotionally intelligent people tend to have better job satisfaction, improved leadership skills, and enhanced work performance. Here's how EQ plays out in the professional landscape:

Leadership Excellence: Exceptional leaders often exhibit high levels of emotional intelligence. They can harness their emotions and understand others' feelings to inspire, resolve conflicts, and create a positive work environment.

Teamwork: Emotional intelligence fosters cooperative attitudes and encourages constructive feedback, both of which contribute to effective teamwork.

Improved Performance: Emotional intelligence can help individuals manage stress effectively, approach challenges proactively, and maintain motivation, all of which substantially contribute to improved performance and job satisfaction.

Understanding and developing emotional intelligence is a lifelong journey of personal and professional evolution. Through introspection, mindfulness, empathy, and practice, individuals can hone their EQ to foster better relationships, enhance decision-making abilities, and augment both personal growth and professional success.

Chapter 10. Turning Skills into Success: From Theory to Practice

Cultivating skills and knowledge is just one half of personal success; the other half lies in the effective application of those abilities. This journey starts with an understanding of the essential skills, improving on them, and then transforming these skills into discernible success. In this chapter, we'll navigate together through the tangible ways you can turn skills into success, starting from theory and stretching into practice.

10.1. Understanding Skill Application

Skill application is more than just the practical use of abilities learned; it's about harnessing and directing those abilities towards a predetermined goal. To turn skills into tangible success, a deep understanding and acceptance of the skills is required. Here, an in-depth analysis of your skills is performed, and a strategic understanding on how to apply them is developed. This process includes understanding the extent and limits of your skills, recognizing when and where they can be used, and having the courage to apply them when necessary.

10.2. Skill Development- The Theoretical Foundation

Although it's critical to be proactive and apply your skills practically, it's impossible to move into the application stage without first understanding the theory behind a particular skill. Every skill is founded on a set of theories, assumptions, principles, or rules that guide its development and use.

Understanding theoretical knowledge offers multiple benefits. It provides a foundation for developing higher-order skills. It prompts you to engage in critical thinking, builds your communication skills, makes the learning process more efficient, enables you to connect the dots, and ignites curiosity and exploration. By challenging you to engage in cognitive thinking, theory offers a solid base for later application.

10.3. From Theory to Practice: Stages of Skill Development

There are four main stages.

1. Unconscious incompetence: You don't comprehend the skill and your deficiency in this area.

2. Conscious incompetence: You now understand your deficiency but still lack the skill.

3. Conscious competence: With deliberate effort, you've gained the skill.

4. Unconscious competence: The skill now comes as a second nature, with little to no conscious thought.

Recognizing these stages in your skill development process can enable you to focus on areas requiring improvement and adapt your learning strategies accordingly.

10.4. Practical implementation of Skills

Once you have a theoretical understanding of your desired skill and have developed it, the next step is to apply it practically. Find opportunities where you can apply your skills, whether as part of your job, a hobby, or in day-to-day situations. The more you successfully apply the skill, the more confidence you will gain in your abilities, which is often the key ingredient in turning skills into success.

10.5. Leveraging Skills for Success

Once you're comfortable with your skill, the next and final step is to leverage it for success. This can involve looking for opportunities where your skill is in high demand and showing how your abilities help meet these needs better than others.

Remember that success is often subjective, so your definition of success may be different than someone else's. Take steps to define what success looks like for you and use this as your guide.

10.6. Final Thoughts

Empowering yourself with skills is one of the greatest investments you can make. Not only does it provide better occupational and personal opportunities, but it also gives you the tools to mold and direct your life according to your values and aspirations.

The journey from skill acquisition to skill application can be long and challenging. But it is a path worthwhile, leading toward self-improvement, satisfaction, and success. The better you become at applying your skills in a plethora of different situations, the more successful you become.

Remember, skills don't turn into success overnight. It's a gradual process that demands regular practice, patience, and perseverance. It's important to celebrate small victories along the way, as every step forward marks an advancement in your journey of personal growth. So, keep learning, keep improving, keep applying, and remember — success is achievable!

Chapter 11. The Future Self: Crafting Your Personal Roadmap

The journey we embark on when we decide to invest in ourselves begins with the understanding that our future is a realm that's yet to be designed. It's only by evolving our understanding of the 'self', embracing reflection, and leveraging the tools available to us for personal growth that we can journey towards an envisioned future self.

11.1. The Power of Reflection

To craft your personal roadmap, one must first fully understand their current position. Self-reflection is the cornerstone of self-awareness. It assists you in ascertaining your strengths, weaknesses, passions, values, and the situations that stir your creative juices. The genesis of personal growth is the ability to sit with oneself and reflect on interests, aspirations, interactions, and reactions.

Take intentional time each day to engage in reflective practices such as journaling, meditation, introspection or self-questioning. This practice will help you identify trends and patterns in your thoughts, emotions, and behaviors.

11.2. Understanding Your Strengths and Weaknesses

To chart the course toward your future self, you will need to leverage your strengths and acknowledge your weaknesses. Identify what you do well. What tasks seem to flow effortlessly for you? Where have others complimented your skills or abilities? These are likely indicators of your strengths.

Conversely, understand where your weaknesses lie. A weakness is not a flaw, it is merely an area for growth and development. Is there a common task or situation that you often find challenging? Are there particular skills or abilities you've considered improving?

Once identified, focus on enhancing your strengths while also designating time and energy towards improving your weaknesses. Remember, personal growth and evolution are not linear. They involve cycles of learning, practice, and improvement.

11.3. Crafting Your Vision

Now, with an understanding of your current state, dream about your future self. Paint a picture in your mind of who you want to become. Envision the skills, knowledge, values, and perspectives this future self embodies. Crafting this vision provides direction, a crucial aspect of building a personal roadmap.

Consider using visualization techniques to solidify your vision. Create a vision board, write a detailed description, or practice meditation focused on your future self. The more real and tangible your vision becomes in your mind, the more likely you are to manifest it in reality.

11.4. Setting SMART Goals

To transform your future self from a mere vision to achievable reality, SMART goals set the stage. SMART, an acronym for Specific, Measurable, Achievable, Relevant, Time-bound, has become a popular tool for setting and achieving aims.

Establish goals pertinent to the development of your future self. Each goal should have a clear plan indicating how it will be accomplished, by when, and how progress will be measured.

11.5. Building Resilience and Adaptability

As you commence on the journey towards your future self, understand that obstacles are inevitable. However, with resilience and adaptability, you can overcome anything that stands in your path. Resilience is the competence to bounce back from adversity while adaptability is your ability to adjust quickly to change.

Begin by building your mental and emotional resilience. Focus on fostering a positive mindset, engage in mindful practices such as meditation or yoga, maintain physical health and fitness, and surround yourself with positive, supportive individuals.

Secondly, embrace change. Adopt a growth mindset, being open to new experiences and challenges, all while displaying a keen appetite for learning.

11.6. Lifelong Learning

The journey to your future self demands a commitment to lifelong learning. Your commitment to continuously developing new skills and accumulating knowledge is a valuable investment in your personal growth.

Whether you engage in reading, online courses, workshops, or traditional academic programs, keep feeding your curiosity. Expand your horizons and don't limit your learning to one field or area. Remember, every bit of knowledge and every skill acquired plays a part in shaping your future self.

By reflecting on your current self, understanding your strengths and weaknesses, visualizing your future self, setting SMART goals, building resilience and adaptability, and embracing lifelong learning, you're well on your way to crafting your personal roadmap. Yes, the journey will pose challenges, but with your sights set on the horizon of your future self, every step forward is a steppingstone to growth, development, and extraordinary potential of who you could become. Remember, the power to shape your future is within you. Walk the path with courage, perseverance, and an unquenchable desire for self-improvement.